GREAT
AMERICAN PRESIDENTS

WOODROW
WILSON

GREAT
AMERICAN PRESIDENTS

JOHN ADAMS

JOHN QUINCY ADAMS

JIMMY CARTER

THOMAS JEFFERSON

JOHN F. KENNEDY

ABRAHAM LINCOLN

RONALD REAGAN

FRANKLIN DELANO ROOSEVELT

THEODORE ROOSEVELT

HARRY S. TRUMAN

GEORGE WASHINGTON

WOODROW WILSON

GREAT
AMERICAN PRESIDENTS

WOODROW
WILSON

CONTRA COSTA COUNTY LIBRARY

ANN GAINES

FOREWORD BY
WALTER CRONKITE

CHELSEA HOUSE
PUBLISHERS
A Haights Cross Communications Company

CHELSEA HOUSE PUBLISHERS

VP, NEW PRODUCT DEVELOPMENT Sally Cheney
DIRECTOR OF PRODUCTION Kim Shinners
CREATIVE MANAGER Takeshi Takahashi
MANUFACTURING MANAGER Diann Grasse

STAFF FOR WOODROW WILSON

ASSOCIATE EDITOR Kate Sullivan
PRODUCTION ASSISTANT Megan Emery
PHOTO EDITOR Sarah Bloom
SERIES DESIGNER Keith Trego
COVER DESIGNER Keith Trego
LAYOUT 21st Century Publishing and Communications, Inc.

www.chelseahouse.com

First Printing

1 3 5 7 9 8 6 4 2

Library of Congress Cataloging-in-Publication Data

Gaines, Ann.
 Woodrow Wilson / by Ann Gaines.
    p. cm. — (Great American presidents)
Includes bibliographical references and index.
Contents: Vision for peace — Youth, 1856-1875 — Academic career, 1875-1909 — Rise
to the presidency, 1909-1916 — Allied hero, 1914-1921
— Global legacy.
 ISBN 0-7910-7597-4 — ISBN 0-7910-7783-7 (pbk.)
 1. Wilson, Woodrow, 1856-1924—Juvenile literature. 2. Presidents—United States—
Biography—Juvenile literature. [1. Wilson, Woodrow, 1856-1924. 2. Presidents.] I. Title.
II. Series.
 E767.G15 2003
 973.91'3'092—dc21

2003013675

TABLE of CONTENTS

FOREWORD:
WALTER CRONKITE   6

1 VISION FOR PEACE   10

2 YOUTH: 1856–1875   18

3 ACADEMIC CAREER: 1875–1909   30

4 RISE TO THE PRESIDENCY: 1909–1916   44

5 ALLIED HERO: 1914–1921   56

6 GLOBAL LEGACY   76

TIMELINE: THE PRESIDENTS OF THE UNITED STATES   84

PRESIDENTIAL FACT FILE   86

PRESIDENT WILSON IN PROFILE   89

CHRONOLOGY   90

BIBLIOGRAPHY   92

FURTHER READING   93

INDEX   94

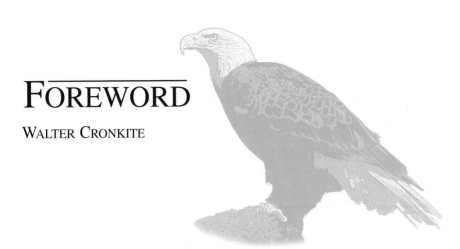

FOREWORD

WALTER CRONKITE

A candle can defy the darkness. It need not have the power of a great searchlight to be a welcome break from the gloom of night. So it goes in the assessment of leadership. He who lights the candle may not have the skill or imagination to turn the light that flickers for a moment into a perpetual glow, but history will assign credit to the degree it is due.

Some of our great American presidents may have had a single moment that bridged the chasm between the ordinary and the exceptional. Others may have assured their lofty place in our history through the sum total of their accomplishments.

When asked who were our greatest presidents, we cannot fail to open our list with the Founding Fathers who put together this nation and nursed it through the difficult years of its infancy. George Washington, John Adams, Thomas Jefferson, and James Madison took the high principles of the revolution against British tyranny and turned the concept of democracy into a nation that became the beacon of hope to oppressed peoples around the globe.

Almost invariably we add to that list our wartime presidents—Abraham Lincoln, perhaps Woodrow Wilson, and certainly Franklin Delano Roosevelt.

Nonetheless there is a thread of irony that runs through the inclusion of the names of those wartime presidents: In many aspects their leadership was enhanced by the fact that, without objection from the people, they assumed extraordinary powers to pursue victory over the nation's enemies (or, in the case of Lincoln, the Southern states).

The complexities of the democratic procedures by which the United States Constitution deliberately tried to withhold unchecked power from the presidency encumbered the presidents who needed their hands freed of the entangling bureaucracy that is the federal government.

Much of our history is written far after the events themselves took place. History may be amended by a much later generation seeking a precedent to justify an action considered necessary at the latter time. The history, in a sense, becomes what later generations interpret it to be.

President Jefferson in 1803 negotiated the purchase of vast lands in the south and west of North America from the French. The deal became knows as the Louisiana Purchase. A century and a half later, to justify seizing the nation's steel mills that were being shut down by a labor strike, President Truman cited the Louisiana Purchase as a case when the president in a major matter ignored Congress and acted almost solely on his own authority.

The case went to the Supreme Court, which overturned Truman six to three. The chief justice, Fred Vinson, was one of the three justices who supported the president. Many historians, however, agreed with the court's majority, pointing out that Jefferson scarcely acted alone: Members of Congress were in the forefront of the agitation to consummate the Louisiana Purchase and Congress voted to fund it.

With more than two centuries of history and precedent now behind us, the Constitution is still found to be flexible when honest and sincere individuals support their own causes with quite different readings of it. These are the questions that end up for interpretation by the Supreme Court.

As late as the early years of the twenty-first century, perhaps the most fateful decision any president ever can make—to commit the nation to war—was again debated and precedent ignored. The Constitution says that only the Congress has the authority to declare war. Yet the Congress, with the objection of few members, ignored this Constitutional provision and voted to give President George W. Bush the right to take the United States to war whenever and under whatever conditions he decided.

Thus a president's place in history may well be determined by how much power he seizes or is granted in re-interpreting and circumventing the remarkable document that is the Constitution. Although the Founding Fathers thought they had spelled out the president's authority in their clear division of powers between the branches of the executive, the legislative and the judiciary, their wisdom has been challenged frequently by ensuing generations. The need and the demand for change is dictated by the march of events, the vast alterations in society, the global condition beyond our influence, and the progress of technology far beyond the imaginations of any of the generations which preceded them.

The extent to which the powers of the presidency will be enhanced and utilized by the chief executives to come in large degree will depend, as they have throughout our history, on the character of the presidents themselves. The limitations on those powers, in turn, will depend on the strength and will of those other two legs of the three-legged stool of American government—the legislative and the judiciary.

And as long as this nation remains a democracy, the final say will rest with an educated electorate in perpetual exercise of its constitutional rights to free speech and a free and alert press.

1

VISION FOR WORLD PEACE

WOODROW WILSON, THE 28th president of the United States, received the Nobel Peace Prize for 1919. The Nobel Peace Prize, one of the most famous and prestigious awards in the world, is given to individuals who have dedicated themselves to the cause of establishing peace, often by negotiating between hostile groups or by creating the means by which achieving peace is possible. When Wilson was honored with this recognition, he became a member of a very distinguished group of intellectuals and activists.

The Nobel committee selected Wilson for two reasons. First, Wilson was honored with the Nobel Peace Prize for his famous Fourteen Points program, a plan he had devised before the end of

This cartoon from 1919 depicts Wilson presenting the League of Nations as an olive branch (a symbolic offering of peace) to the dove of peace. Although Wilson won the Nobel Peace Prize for his efforts to ensure a lasting peace after World War I, the United States Senate did not support the organization and never ratified the treaty that made the league possible.

World War I so that the war would end with a just and lasting peace. As his last point, he had stated that the world desperately needed a League of Nations, an international association of countries that could help resolve disputes around the world. He also received the prize because of his efforts to include a clause agreeing to the formation of a

League of Nations in the terms of the Treaty of Versailles, which officially ended World War I.

Woodrow Wilson was proud to be chosen for this great honor. The prize was awarded in Oslo, Norway, on December 20, 1920. However, due to political unrest in the world, Wilson was unable to accept his award in person, which disappointed him greatly. Although Wilson remained in Washington, D.C., American diplomat Albert G. Schmedeman attended the ceremony on Wilson's behalf and read aloud a short message from him. In it, Wilson emphasized his sincere belief that it would take tremendous effort to keep peace in the world. He said, "I am moved not only by a profound gratitude for the recognition of my [sincere and] earnest efforts in the cause of peace, but also by a very poignant humility before the vastness of the work still called for by this cause."

Sadly, receiving the Nobel Peace Prize was one of the few happy moments Woodrow Wilson enjoyed in the last years of his life. Only a year earlier, he was at the pinnacle of his short-lived political career, experiencing immense popularity around the world. This status had quickly faded.

In fact, until 1909, Wilson was not a politician but an academic, a man of books. After years as a college professor, he had become the president of Princeton University, one of the most prestigious colleges in the nation. Impressed by this quiet man who seemed to blaze to life when he stepped up to a podium to speak, the leaders of New Jersey's Democratic Party asked him to run for the office of governor in 1910. In the two years he spent as governor, he accomplished so much, especially for workers, that he gained a favorable national reputation.

The Democrats chose Wilson to run for president in 1912, and he won. In his first term as president, he devoted almost all of his attention to domestic affairs, spending more time on matters inside the country than on what occurred elsewhere in the world. In doing so, he acted similarly to most of the presidents who had preceded him. As a group, they had wanted the United States to remain apart from the rest of the world: It was only after the Spanish–American War of 1898 that anyone thought of the United States as a superpower, a nation so strong that it could dictate what happened in other parts of the world.

During Wilson's first term in office, he concentrated on pushing Congress to pass reform laws that affected the American economy and workers' lives. World War I started in the middle of his first term. Great Britain, France, and Russia honored secret treaties they had made earlier and went to war against Austria–Hungary and Germany in order to prevent both countries from expanding. For more than two years, Wilson was steadfast in his belief that the United States should stay out of World War I. In fact, he won his second campaign for president, in 1916, largely because he was known as "the man who had kept the country out of war." Just after taking his second inaugural oath, however, he became convinced that America had to intervene in the war: Germany would not stop sinking ships carrying Americans.

After Wilson asked Congress to declare war on Germany, America mobilized quickly, sending weapons and two

Wilson asked Congress to declare war on Germany on April 2, 1917. He had kept the United States out of the war for two years, but when German actions became increasingly hostile toward American civilians, he realized that the United States had to join the war effort.

million soldiers, sailors, and air force pilots to fight in Europe. The late but substantial American involvement in the war helped bring it to a rapid close. As the end drew near, Wilson called on his mighty intellect and knowledge of history and government as he thought about what was necessary for peace.

In 1919, Germany was finally forced to ask for an armistice, admitting it could fight no more and had lost the war. Wilson became the first American president to go to Europe while in office when he sailed to France to attend the peace conference that followed. At the time of his departure, most Americans were extremely proud of him. On his arrival in Europe, he discovered that he was considered a hero there, too, as great crowds gathered to cheer him.

By the time Wilson was selected for the Nobel Peace Prize, however, his popularity had drastically decreased. He had not been able to achieve all that he hoped in Europe; despite his best efforts, France and Great Britain had insisted that Germany be punished harshly for its actions in the war. According to the Treaty of Versailles, which Germany was forced to sign, the nation was not only out-lawed from opening many new factories and building up its military, but it had to agree to pay reparations—fines so huge that they would cripple Germany's economy.

> "... [Mankind] has not yet been rid of the unspeakable horror of war. I am convinced that our generation has, despite its wounds, made notable progress. But it is the better part of wisdom to consider our work as one begun. It will be a continuing labor. In the indefinite course of [the] years before us there will be abundant opportunity for others to distinguish themselves in the crusade against hate and fear and war."
>
> —Woodrow Wilson, Nobel Prize Acceptance Speech, 1920

Wilson had succeeded in his main goal: establishing the League of Nations. Back in the United States, however, Wilson was extremely disappointed that he could not persuade America's political leaders that the United States should ratify the Treaty of Versailles, which would make the country a member of the League of Nations. In fact, Wilson ruined his health by undertaking an exhausting cross-country train trip to meet ordinary Americans, talking to them about why he believed so strongly that they should push their representatives to vote in favor of the treaty and thus

PRESIDENT WILSON'S LEGACY

The United Nations

The idea of an international association of countries with the purpose of maintaining peace around the world came from Woodrow Wilson. At the end of World War I, he pushed for the creation of what he called the League of Nations and was very involved in its founding, helping to write the league's covenant in 1919. He believed that its primary function should be collective security, meaning that its members would pledge to help any other member that came under attack.

Not only did Wilson fail to persuade America's political leaders that the United States should join the league, but he also would have been grievously disappointed, had he lived, to see how rapidly the league's powerful members began to disagree over its purpose. France, for example, believed that its most important job was not collective security, but instead keeping Germany from rebuilding its military or trying to take back territory it had lost as a result of the war. Germany, which never joined the league, always criticized the league because Germany's leaders, too, believed that its primary purpose was to keep their nation down.

In the long run, the League of Nations was a terrible failure. Although it did have some success keeping small nations from starting wars, it had very little effect when a powerful nation was involved. There were instances in which its powerful members attacked other members. The last came in 1935, when Italy attacked Ethiopia. By this time, many members had already withdrawn from the league. When other powerful members like Great Britain and France did not assist Ethiopia, the league stopped functioning completely. It was formally dissolved in 1946.

One very good thing came out of the League of Nations' experience, however. The United Nations was founded in April 1946 to replace it. That body, which in 2002 had 191 members, has been much more successful in making the world a more peaceful place by instilling peacekeeping forces in hostile areas, negotiating between disagreeing parties, and overseeing the disarmament of countries with huge stores of weaponry. In many ways, it is Woodrow Wilson's most notable legacy.

the league. Historian Gene Smith believes that Wilson was well on his way to bringing the public around to his point of view when suddenly, midway through his tour, he collapsed from exhaustion. He was soon diagnosed as having suffered a massive stroke, which left him unable to speak or write clearly.

A broken man, he lost all influence on American politics, and the United States never ratified the treaty. Smith regards this as one of the greatest calamities in American history, writing, "Had the United States entered the League—and who can doubt that if Wilson had retained all his faculties in full vigor it would have done so?—how much brighter might have been the ensuing years!" Smith speculates that if the United States had signed the treaty, Hitler might not have been able to come to power in Germany and thus World War II could have been prevented.

Wilson spent his final year in the White House a lonely and bitter man. The business of government went on without him. Once he had hoped to run for a third term, but of course he did not. Republican Warren G. Harding became the next president. When Wilson died—only three years after leaving office—his reputation remained tarnished. Today, however, Wilson's foresight, intellect, and dedication to the establishment of enduring peace is recognized in America and the world at large. A great mind and a great leader, Woodrow Wilson made an enormous mark on not only the United States but the entire world.

2

YOUTH:
1856–1875

THOMAS WOODROW WILSON was born in Staunton, Virginia, on December 28, 1856, to Joseph Ruggles and Janet Woodrow Wilson. He was the Wilson family's third child, after sisters Marion and Annie, and the first son. A brother, Joseph Jr., was born in 1867. Tommy or Tommie, as he was called by friends and family until he went to college, grew up in a close-knit family during a difficult time in American history. His parents seem to have had a happy marriage, perhaps in part because they came from similar backgrounds: Both sides of his family had roots in Scotland and belonged to the Presbyterian church.

Joseph Wilson's parents, James Wilson and Mary Anne Adams,

Thomas Woodrow Wilson was born on December 28, 1856, in this house in Staunton, Virginia, where Wilson's father was the head of a private school and a church. The family moved to Georgia a few years later and remained in the South, where they witnessed the horrors of the Civil War.

emigrated from Scotland as young, single adults around 1807. They married the following year and settled down in Philadelphia, where James became a printer and newspaper publisher. A few years later, the family moved west, to Ohio, which was then still on the frontier. Joseph's oldest brother followed in their father's footsteps, eventually becoming editor of the *Chicago Tribune*. Joseph himself shared his family's love of reading and writing but pursued a different career path: He went to a seminary and became a Presbyterian minister.

Janet Wilson, Tommy's mother, was nicknamed Jessie. Born in Scotland, she came with her family to the United States while she was still a very young girl. After living in Canada for a short time, her family settled in Ohio. Like Joseph Wilson, Jessie's father, Thomas Woodrow, was a Presbyterian minister. Both he and her brother were thinkers by nature and learned men. When Jessie married Joseph in 1849, she easily adopted her new role as a minister's wife.

Joseph and Jessie were quite different in terms of personality. They were both outgoing, but whereas Joseph was also proud and could be demanding and stern, Jessie had a softer side. A warm, affectionate woman, she liked to take care of people, a quality that helped her in her duties as a minister's wife. She helped Joseph tend his parish, and frequently found herself called upon by church members for words of advice and gifts of food. Both she and Joseph had a deep and abiding Christian faith, which they passed on to all of their children.

Soon after their marriage, the Wilsons moved to Virginia. In moving from the Midwest to the South, they experienced a very different way of life. In the 1850s, slavery was a very controversial issue in the United States. In the North, there were many abolitionists, who wanted to see slavery outlawed. In the South, supporters of slavery vastly outnumbered abolitionists. Owners of both huge plantations and smaller farms depended on slaves to grow the South's most profitable crops: Cotton and tobacco are both very labor-intensive and required a lot of people working hard in their fields.

To his family's dismay, Joseph Wilson took the side of the South as the Civil War neared. In the words of historian Arthur Walworth, he "accepted the political views of his parishioners," meaning that he agreed with them that the United States government interfered too much in states' affairs. The federal government made some decisions (as in the case of slavery) that Southerners believed were the right of individual states to make.

When Tommy was born, his father was in charge of a Presbyterian private school for girls and a church in the small town of Staunton, Virginia. The family lived in the church rectory. In 1860, the Wilsons moved to Augusta, Georgia, where Joseph took over the First Presbyterian Church. They lived there until 1870. Their stay in Augusta encompassed some of the most tumultuous years in American history—those of the Civil War and its immediate aftermath.

THE CIVIL WAR

In 1861, eleven Southern states seceded from the Union to form the Confederate States of America. Joseph Wilson believed they were right to do so. When the American Presbyterian Church followed suit and split in two, he became a high-ranking official in the new Southern sect.

Very difficult years followed for those who lived in the Confederacy. Southern men—and boys—joined the

Confederate army in great numbers and marched off to fight, and there were even cases of women who felt so strongly about the cause that they disguised themselves as men so they could also enlist.

The Civil War was one of the bloodiest wars in all of human history. Soldiers died by the hundreds of thousands on both sides. Many of those who made it through the war returned home hideously maimed or close to starving (conditions in prisoner of war camps were horrible). The women and children that the soldiers left behind had also suffered. Wives had to take over their husbands' farms and businesses. Families had to go without, sometimes lacking basic necessities like food or shoes.

Many Civil War battles took place on Southern soil; by the end of the war, much of the South had been destroyed, its land damaged by the fighting. In 1864, almost 100,000 Union soldiers marched into the Wilsons' home state, Georgia, under General Sherman. After a long period of fighting, they finally captured the city of Atlanta, which by that time was burned in many places, on September 2, 1864.

Because their father did not go off to fight, the Wilson children escaped some of the fear and heartache many other Confederate children suffered. Still, they saw the terror and despair that afflicted the South. Later in life, Woodrow Wilson remembered how at age three he had learned hard times were coming: He had overheard grown-ups angry over the election of Abraham Lincoln as president of the United States predict, "There'll be war!" As a little boy, he once saw Robert E. Lee, the famous

Jefferson Davis was the president of the Confederate States of America during the Civil War. The war had a profound impact on Wilson when he was a child in Georgia; he witnessed many disturbing events during the war, including President Davis being led through the street in chains after the war ended.

Confederate general, up close because his father's church was used for a time to house a makeshift hospital for wounded Confederate soldiers.

When the war ended in 1865, Tommy was nine years old. He was present when Confederate president Jefferson Davis—who had been captured after he fled for Mexico when Lee surrendered to Union general Ulysses S. Grant—was led through Atlanta in chains on his way to Fortress Monroe, where he was imprisoned. Wilson never forgot this moment, which he considered extremely sad and disturbing.

RECONSTRUCTION

The South continued to suffer during the period known as Reconstruction, which lasted from 1865 to 1877. Grant had promised Lee that those who had fought on the side of the Confederacy would not be treated as traitors. In most other countries, rebels who lost a civil war would have been shot or hanged. Nevertheless, the North did not easily forgive the Confederates: The federal government imposed strict rules and regulations on the South, making every Confederate state demonstrate that it had been reformed or reconstructed before it was formally readmitted to the Union. President Andrew Johnson sent the Union army back into the South to enforce martial law. For a time, soldiers occupied Joseph Wilson's church, using it as barracks. Wilson, like other former Confederates, had no choice; he had to allow them to do what they wanted.

During Reconstruction, Tommy and his siblings saw many sad sights. They watched defeated soldiers go through their town, slowly making their way on foot back to the homes they hoped still stood. They met women and children who had lost their plantations or farms when Union soldiers burned their land. There was also a large population of now-homeless former slaves. These people reveled in their emancipation—their freedom—but their lot remained hard because few people could afford to hire them to do the work they had done as slaves. Despite all this, Tommy had a happy childhood. His own family remained safe and secure and always hopeful that the future held better things.

A SCHOLAR'S BEGINNING

Like many children who lived in the South during the Civil War, Tommy received a haphazard education. He never had much formal schooling; when he was a small boy, his parents taught him at home. His father was in charge of most lessons, and although Joseph Wilson was a good teacher and tried very hard, he failed to teach Tommy to read. Nevertheless, he did not give up on his son's education.

Because Tommy could not read for himself, Joseph Wilson often read out loud from the Bible, as well as storybooks, newspapers, and magazines. He also took Tommy on what were essentially field trips so Tommy could see for himself things like how flour was made at a mill. Joseph also coached him in public speaking, teaching Tommy to express himself clearly in front of an audience. Thanks to his father's efforts, Tommy became a very skilled orator, as well as a debater (someone skilled in making arguments) over the years.

In August of 1867, when Tommy started to attend a private school, he still could not read very well. His teachers labeled him slow; modern historians believe that he suffered from dyslexia (a disturbance in the ability to read), a condition that was not understood at that time. He received low grades in school largely because of this inability to read.

When Tommy was 13 years old, the Wilson family moved once more, this time to Columbia, South Carolina. There, Joseph Wilson taught at a theological seminary and preached at the local church. Tommy still received most of his education from his family, although he also had formal lessons in Latin and Greek.

As a teenager, Tommy started to read more easily and greatly enjoyed losing himself in the adventure stories of his day. He daydreamed about being an admiral in the navy and sailing around fighting pirates. As his writing skills improved, he thought it was fun to create fake reports to the government about his feats, describing in great detail the brave battles and wily escapes he imagined.

> "I lived in a dream life when I was a lad and even now my thought goes back for refreshment to those days when all the world seemed to me a place of heroic adventure."
>
> —Woodrow Wilson, reflecting on his childhood

Tommy had other interests as a teenager. He played baseball on a local team. His religious faith was so important to him that he applied on his own for adult membership in the Presbyterian Church at a very early age. At the same time, he started to read books and magazines about politics given to him by his father. He developed a fascination with the British parliamentary system in particular.

In the fall of 1873, Tommy Wilson was quickly nearing adulthood and was almost fully grown. Always very tall and

Wilson enrolled at Davidson College in North Carolina in 1873, perhaps to become a Presbyterian minister like his father. Unfortunately, health problems forced him to leave before he completed his second year.

thin compared to his peers, at 16 years of age, Wilson had short, dark hair and did not need glasses. In terms of personality, he was much as he would be in later years: In private, he was given to daydreaming and emotional outbursts, but in public, he was almost always focused and serious. He excelled at public speaking; thanks to his skill as a speaker, he would later develop a reputation for being a charismatic man who could persuade others to his point of view.

Tommy enrolled at Davidson College, a Presbyterian college in North Carolina, perhaps because his parents expected him to become a minister like his father. Tommy stayed for all of his freshman year but did not finish his sophomore year. He had to leave campus because of what a doctor described as "nervous indigestion," an ailment he would suffer from off and on until he reached the White House. When he left college, Tommy went back to the house in Columbia but soon moved with his family to Wilmington, North Carolina. His father had resigned from his job at the Columbia seminary in a huff because his church had hired another preacher without his consent. When this happened, Joseph Wilson told his students that they were not allowed to attend the church anymore and that they could only worship at services he held at their school. They refused, and Joseph became so furious that he left.

While recuperating, Tommy spent an enormous amount of time with his father. They resumed reading together, indulging their common interests in philosophy, politics, and religion.

SERIOUS STUDY BEGINS

By the fall of 1875, Tommy felt well enough to return to his studies. He did not go back to Davidson (historians are not sure why) but went instead to the College of New Jersey, which later changed its name to Princeton University. Many students went to this college to study to become Presbyterian ministers. Tommy began undergoing significant changes at this new school. He became a notable scholar. At Davidson, his grades had been mediocre at best, and they remained so in his first year at the College of New Jersey. In his second year, however, Tommy began to shine as a student. He made it onto the honor roll and stayed there.

At some point, he decided not to train for the ministry and instead followed his interest in politics, joining a political club whose members gathered for heated discussions concerning the U.S. Constitution and so forth. He helped found a new debate society. He authored articles on Otto von Bismarck, who had been chancellor of the nation of Prussia, which would later become Germany, and William Pitt the Elder, who was one of Britain's greatest political leaders,

"That is Gladstone, the greatest statesman that ever lived. I intend to be a statesman, too."

—Woodrow Wilson reportedly said this as a boy of 16 while looking at a portrait of William Gladstone, Britain's popular prime minister

for the undergraduate magazine. He also edited a campus magazine and served as president of the baseball association.

In his senior year, Wilson was well known and respected by his classmates. He wrote his required thesis on "Cabinet Government in the United States." This paper was accepted for publication as an article in the respected *International Review* magazine.

Nearing graduation, he daydreamed of one day being elected to the U.S. Senate from Virginia, but the time had not yet come for him actively to pursue a political career. When he graduated from the College of New Jersey, he enrolled in law school at the University of Virginia.

3

ACADEMIC CAREER: 1875–1909

WOODROW WILSON DECIDED to go to law school because he thought that being a lawyer would help him in a career as a politician. As he later wrote to his future wife Ellen Axson, "The profession I chose was politics; the profession I entered was law. I entered the one because I thought it would lead to the other. It was once the sure road; and Congress is still full of lawyers."

He enrolled in law school in the fall of 1879 under the name Thomas W. Wilson. By the start of the next year, however, he always introduced himself and signed his name as Woodrow. At the University of Virginia as at the College of New Jersey, he was a good student who also made plenty of time for fun. He umpired baseball games and wrote for the university magazine. He joined a debate society. Midway during his second year, he again became ill. He left school again, although this time he took his coursework home. When he completed the work required, the law school granted him a degree in absentia. Once he passed the bar exam (the test required to become a lawyer), he opened a law office in Atlanta, Georgia, with a friend from school. Their business did not flourish, however, mostly because Atlanta already had a large number of lawyers.

In 1883, on a trip to Rome, Georgia, Wilson made the acquaintance of Ellen Axson, a Presbyterian minister's daughter, and they began a relationship. He liked to express his emotions, which he often kept inside, to her.

He used the time he did not spend working or visiting Ellen to write. He wrote articles on congressional government and Georgia's convict lease system (in which convicts were "leased" to wealthy farmers and others to perform what was often much like slave labor) and sent them to magazines, but they were rejected. Another article, on cabinet government, was accepted by *Overland Monthly*.

A NEW CAREER

In the summer of 1883, Wilson proposed to Ellen. Their engagement would last two years. By the fall, he realized that he did not like being a lawyer. He found the work dull.

Wilson decided to go back to school. He had a new

Wilson met Ellen Axson, a child of a Presbyterian minister like himself, on a trip to Rome, Georgia. Although Wilson often found it difficult to express his emotions to others, he revealed them to Ellen. After a two-year courtship, the couple married in June 1885.

goal: to become a university professor. His father gave him the money to start a doctorate program in history at Johns Hopkins University.

At Johns Hopkins, Wilson continued to enjoy the extracurricular activities universities have to offer, such as singing in the glee club and, as always, debating. He also continued work on the piece he had written on congressional government, revising and expanding it until it became book-length. He and a friend started to write a history of economic thought in the United States, as well.

In the spring of 1885, after Wilson had been studying on the Johns Hopkins campus for two years, he left to get a job teaching and to write his dissertation. This was a very exciting time for him. First, his book *Congressional Government* was published and received very positive reviews. Then, in June, he and Ellen married and went on a honeymoon in the mountains of North Carolina. When they came back, he accepted a teaching job at Bryn Mawr College, a new women's college near Philadelphia. Neither he nor Ellen displayed a great commitment to the cause of higher education for women, but he was glad to take the job because it paid well and allowed him time for his own studies. He would stay there for two years, during which Ellen gave birth to two girls, the first, Margaret, in 1886 and the second, Jessie, in 1887. Their family expanded when one of Ellen's brothers and then a cousin came to live with them.

> *"I have a passion for interpreting great thoughts to the world. It is my heart's dearest desire that I may become one of the guides of public policy."*
> — Woodrow Wilson, during his career as a professor

According to university rules, Woodrow Wilson was supposed to return to Johns Hopkins after he finished writing his dissertation to take oral examinations before he was awarded his doctorate degree. In the spring of 1886, he wrote to his professors to plead that he "always cut a sorry figure" in such situations, becoming nervous and tongue-tied. The professors agreed to make an exception for him, so he took five written examinations and then participated in an "interview," in which he discussed his work rather than being quizzed on facts he had learned while in graduate school. He apparently did well, because the university awarded him his doctorate. He had become Dr. Wilson.

Wilson did not particularly like teaching the Bryn Mawr women. He complained that although they paid close attention to his lectures, they could do little with the information he gave them other than repeat it back to him. Thinking he might not want to stay at Bryn Mawr, he took a trip to Washington, D.C., with the hope that he might find a position in the government. He introduced himself to the heads of various federal offices, but no one offered him a job.

His disappointment at not finding a government job faded somewhat when a publisher gave him a contract to write a college government textbook entitled *The State*. This he did while continuing to teach at Bryn Mawr. Although this book seems outdated today, it is important because in it Wilson proposes for the first time that international law should govern the nations of the world and suggested an idea that would eventually evolve into the League of Nations.

Wilson was happy when, after being at Bryn Mawr for two years, he was offered a new position at another college, Wesleyan University. He accepted partially because Wesleyan would pay more and because he would teach men. The family moved to Middleton, Connecticut, where Ellen would later give birth to the Wilsons' third daughter, Eleanor.

PRINCETON UNIVERSITY PROFESSOR

Wilson stayed at Wesleyan for two years, from 1888 to 1890, teaching history. As he had hoped, he enjoyed working with the students there. Certainly they liked him—he gained as a reputation as both a fine teacher and a funny man. Yet he found himself thinking of leaving. He began to dream of returning to his alma mater, the College of New Jersey (yet to be named Princeton) to teach public law.

A friend introduced him to the then-president of that school, Dr. Francis L. Patton. Patton told Wilson that what he really needed at the moment was a professor of political economy. He promised that if Wilson would fill that position now, a chair in public law would later be created for him. Wilson refused. Nevertheless, in February 1890, the college wrote to him to say that he could have almost exactly what he wanted—he was offered a position teaching jurisprudence and political economy.

In 1890, Wilson accepted a position as a professor at his alma mater, the College of New Jersey. Wilson quickly became a favorite instructor among the students and eventually was asked to be president of the college.

Wesleyan tried to get Wilson to stay, but he decided to leave, and thus the Wilson family moved again. Wilson became a professor at the College of New Jersey in the fall of 1890. He would remain a professor there for ten years.

PRESIDENT WILSON'S LEGACY

The United States as a Peacekeeper

Woodrow Wilson was teaching at Princeton when the United States intervened in another country's political situation for the first time. President William McKinley declared war on Spain in 1898 because of an incident that occurred in Cuba. Cuba had been a Spanish colony for centuries, but now Cubans fought for their independence. The United States became involved when, on February 15, 1898, the *Maine,* one of its battleships anchored at the port of Havana, exploded. More than 250 American sailors were killed. Americans assumed that it had been blown up by a Spanish bomb (today historians believe a mechanical problem caused the ship's boiler to explode). The United States declared war and set to work destroying the Spanish navy.

For a time after its victory in the Spanish–American war, the United States stepped back and deliberately stayed out of other countries' troubles. During Wilson's presidency, however, he demanded that the nation play an active role as a peacekeeper. He believed that the United States had to lead the rest of the world in doing what is right. For a time after he left office, Americans decided they wanted the United States to lessen its involvement in international affairs. Following Wilson's example, however, President Franklin Roosevelt pushed the United States to be a peacekeeper during and after World War II. Other modern presidents have also believed in the United States as a leader of international peace, a belief Wilson articulated when he said: "I do not mean any disrespect to any other great people, when I say that America is now the hope of the world."

At the same time, Wilson continued to write, this time trying his hand at a new genre. He wrote some literary essays, hoping to "make the sad laugh and take heart again." His writing earned him accolades, as did his public speaking.

Word spread among the student body that Wilson's classes were interesting, and enrollment in them increased. The first year he taught one particular class it had 150 students. Ten years later, there were more than 300 students in that class. He always started his classes by making a short series of statements. He would go over them carefully so that the young men in the lecture hall could write them down word for word. When they finished, he would ask them to put down their pens and listen while he explained to them what he meant. Sometimes he illustrated his points by telling them stories he had recently read in the news. Other times, he pulled lessons from history. According to one of his biographers, Arthur Walworth, "He was at his best in depicting scenes in the age-long battle for free government." Every once in a while, the students were so moved they broke out in cheers! He did more than teach, sponsoring student clubs and even coaching the football team one year. Year after year, the student body elected him professor of the year.

During the time he taught at the College of New Jersey, he was a vocal member of faculty senate. He persuaded his fellow professors that the college should institute the honor system, even though the president argued against it.

In 1893, Wilson spoke at the World's Fair in Chicago. He was well known for his speeches, which were often reprinted, and traveled very far to give them. His ability to communicate his beliefs helped him in his rise to the presidency.

This meant that instead of making a great effort to patrol classrooms and the library, the professors at the college trusted their students not to cheat on tests or copy one another's papers.

During his years at the College of New Jersey, Wilson was invited more and more frequently to deliver speeches to groups outside of Princeton. In doing so, he traveled all up and down the East Coast, and in 1893, he even gave a speech at the World's Fair in Chicago. His speeches were very favorably received and many were reprinted.

In 1896, the board of trustees decided that the College of New Jersey should change its name to Princeton University on the 150th anniversary of its founding. Woodrow Wilson was the honored speaker at the celebration held to mark this milestone in the school's history. He gave a stirring speech, entitled "Princeton in the Nation's Service," in which he talked of his dream of a scholar's paradise, a place where a school interacted with the nation, passing the nation ideas and then helping see those ideas implemented.

> "It is indispensable, it seems to me, if [a college] is to do its right service, that the air of affairs should be admitted to all its classrooms. I do not mean the air of party politics, but the air of the world's transactions, the consciousness of the solidarity of the race, the sense of the duty of man toward man, of the presence of men in every problem, of the significance of truth for guidance as well as for knowledge. . . .
> We dare not keep aloof and closet ourselves. . ."
>
> — Woodrow Wilson in his speech "Princeton in the Nation's Service"

In the meantime, Wilson wrote two history books: one book, entitled *Division and Reunion,* covered the history of politics in America, and the other was a biography of George Washington. His greatest success as an author came when Harper's offered him $12,000 to write a massive history of the United States.

By the end of the 1890s, many students and graduates of Princeton had become unhappy with Patton, the university's president. They noticed that he did not attend many of the school's football games and thought he lacked school spirit. In 1902, a trustee wrote to Patton asking him to resign. He agreed to step down and suggested Woodrow Wilson be asked to take his place. Both students and the young alumni eagerly accepted this suggestion, even though Wilson had little experience as an administrator or in handling money. On the same day the trustees accepted Patton's resignation, they appointed a committee to select his successor.

In a matter of hours, the committee decided to offer the job to Wilson and had gotten the board's unanimous support. Woodrow and Ellen Wilson had known that he might be given the appointment, but they thought that it would only happen after a long and drawn-out process. They were surprised and delighted both at the speed with which the decision had been made and with the news that every single trustee had voted in favor of him.

PRINCETON UNIVERSITY PRESIDENT

Wilson's inauguration as president of Princeton University took place at the end of October of 1900. Among those who came for the occasion were Grover Cleveland, Theodore Roosevelt, J.P. Morgan, Mark Twain, and Booker T. Washington. Wilson delivered yet another impressive speech. One of the people who heard it was a Democratic politician named William Thompson, who decided that Wilson would make a "great candidate." This was not entirely a compliment. Thompson clearly believed that

Wilson was a very powerful speaker, but he also saw Wilson as a weak man and boasted, "Why I could twiddle that man right around my fingers. . . ."

The same month that Wilson took over Princeton, his huge, ten-volume history of the American people appeared. It would go through several editions and be translated into foreign languages and sold abroad. It brought Wilson name recognition across the nation. After it was published, he continued to write, particularly about government.

As president of Princeton University, Wilson was permitted much more power than previous presidents had. The university's trustees gave him the authority to make decisions that they used to make. They later regretted this decision.

Wilson immediately began to propose drastic changes. He wanted to expand the staff of the school by adding 50 preceptors. These people would not be professors but more like the tutors at England's prestigious Oxford University. He also wanted Princeton to add a graduate school, an engineering school, a school of jurisprudence, and a natural history museum. Many of his ideas were accepted, but the student body loudly protested one: He wanted to build new dormitories around quadrangles where both students and faculty would live and eat together. As part of this plan, he proposed eliminating the upperclassmen's eating clubs, which were very much like fraternities. The students hated this idea so much that he finally had to give it up.

Over time, Wilson became unpopular. Before the situation reached the point at which he would have been asked to resign, Wilson left, finally ready to start his political career.

4

RISE TO THE PRESIDENCY: 1909–1916

AT THE BEGINNING of the twentieth century, America was in the throes of change. The United States had become the world's greatest industrial power, with more factories than any other nation on Earth. Its extensive railroad system meant that not only could people travel from one coast to the other in a matter of days, but also that goods were shipped all over the country. Even in small towns, people suddenly had access to many different products. Thomas Edison and other inventors seemed to come out with a new timesaving device every day. Life was becoming easier and progress seemed very apparent.

In the early part of the twentieth century, young children often worked in factories, enduring long hours and harsh conditions. Wilson supported the social reform movement that began around this time to improve the lives of workers, particularly children.

Industrial leaders became household names. As cut-throat competitors, these men cornered their respective markets, forcing their rivals out of business and establishing large companies called trusts. They became enormously wealthy. Some of these men, including Andrew Carnegie and John D. Rockefeller, became philanthropists, giving vast sums of money to charity: Carnegie funded the building of public libraries across the nation, and Rockefeller gave his money to educational institutions.

Ultimately, these men did not share enough of their wealth. They paid their employees very low wages and failed to provide good working conditions. This meant that while captains of industry lived in the lap of luxury, most of their workers led very hard lives. The nation's factories employed hundreds of thousands of unskilled laborers, many of whom were immigrants who just arrived in the United States and spoke little English. Women and children as young as eight filled many factory jobs. The workday was very long—people often worked 12 hours at a stretch—and factories were dangerous places. Gruesome accidents occurred in factories across America every day, but railroad and factory owners fought against the institution of safety laws.

Workers slowly began to join labor unions, cooperatives pledged to help their members achieve higher wages and better working conditions. Between 1881 and 1905, American workers went on strike 37,000 times. These strikes made industrialists furious. They refused to give in to worker demands as often as possible. Some observers believed that class warfare was about to break out in the United States.

A social reform movement began around this time. Reformers wanted not only to help workers but also to improve living conditions in America's rapidly growing cities. Immigrants typically lived in large groups in tiny apartments in big, dirty, dark tenement buildings. People like Jane Addams became more and more concerned about the nation's slums. Some founded settlement houses, social centers in poor neighborhoods that offered classes in English, nursery programs, and a variety of wholesome entertainment including plays and concerts.

New Jersey, one of the most populous states, had more than its share of problems. It had once been a largely agricultural state, but by the time Woodrow Wilson became president of Princeton, it had a great deal of industry and large populations of immigrants and poor people.

At that time, New Jersey's state government was controlled by powerful and corrupt political party organizations known as machines. The Democratic machine wanted to find a man to run for governor who would appeal to the voters and could be easily controlled. George Harvey, the editor of *Harper's Weekly*, suggested to James S. Smith Jr., the Democratic boss of New Jersey, that Wilson would be a good man to have in office. Some historians believe that Wilson accepted the nomination largely because he wanted to get away from Princeton. (Thus he would not have to admit that he had not achieved success at the university because he failed to get approval for some of his grandest schemes.)

A POLITICAL CAREER

Whatever his reasons, Wilson ran for election in 1910. When the announcement was made that he was a candidate, both progressives and labor union leaders spoke out against him, branding him the tool of the party bosses. At the party convention in Trenton in September, after he accepted the nomination, Wilson delivered a speech in which he made it extremely clear that he planned to steer his own course. Wilson pledged that he would "[serve] the people of the State with singleness of purpose." Observers understood that when Wilson said, "Not only have no pledges of any kind been given, but none have been proposed or desired," he meant that he was his own man and did not see himself as owing loyalty to the Democratic leaders of the state.

Within a few weeks Wilson learned how to deliver a good campaign speech. He started out giving what were essentially academic lectures but soon loosened up, adding more personal appeals and talking about specific current issues rather than discussing abstract ideas about how government should work. He dedicated himself to fighting against "special privilege" and spoke constantly about his plans for reform.

In the end, Woodrow Wilson won the election by almost 50,000 votes. He was inaugurated on January 17, 1911. He was also credited with helping so many members of his party get elected that the state legislature went from being Republican to Democratic.

In office, Wilson threw himself into his work and accomplished a great deal. He kept his promises to institute reform. He began to break the hold the political machines had on the state's politics, and his first step was refusing to support long-time Democratic bigwig James E. Smith in a campaign for the U.S. Senate. Wilson instead backed someone new to politics. He also pushed legislators to pass a bill that established a direct primary system, which gave voters more say in who ran for office.

Wilson then went to work trying to reform business in

New Jersey. He created a public utilities commission, which had the authority to set rates and regulate practices so that electric companies, for example, could no longer charge whatever they wanted. He persuaded the state legislature to pass a workmen's compensation law, a piece of legislation that required companies to offer disability payments to employees who had been injured on the job. Wilson also encouraged the state legislature to pass what was known as a corrupt practices act, under which leaders who broke the law were punished much more severely than in the past.

In his second year in office, Wilson devoted a great deal of effort to passing a law that allowed cities to establish new governments with elected city commissioners. All of this brought him a great deal of positive public attention, and his reputation as a good man spread from New Jersey to other places. He did his part to earn that reputation, accepting speaking engagements outside of his state, even though this exposed him to criticism from the people of New Jersey, who wanted him to stay home and take care of business there.

THE 1912 ELECTION

Confident in his own abilities and with the backing of key Democrats, Woodrow Wilson entered the 1912 presidential campaign. This would prove to be one of the most interesting elections in American history because there were two former presidents in the race. The Republican candidate was the incumbent president, William Howard Taft. Taft had been elected in 1908 after serving as governor of Ohio, the governor of the annexed Philippine Islands, and finally as Theodore Roosevelt's secretary of war. A good-natured man, Taft did some positive things as president, especially in terms of breaking up large corporations that held monopolies over particular industries, called trusts. He made mistakes, however, by making enemies of other politicians.

Some Republicans so disliked Taft that when their party nominated him to run for president in 1912, they left the Republican Party. The former Republicans founded a new party, the Progressive Party, which held its convention six weeks later, in August. At the convention, Progressives nominated Theodore Roosevelt, who had been president from 1901 to 1907, to run again. Roosevelt had decided not to run in 1908 because he was tired of the pressures of being president even though he was popular enough to win reelection. In fact, Taft won the 1908 election largely because of Roosevelt's support. Roosevelt spoke highly of Taft during Taft's first year in office, but Roosevelt then went on a long safari in Africa. When Roosevelt returned, he decided that Taft was not doing a very good job as president and that he himself should run again. Roosevelt gladly accepted the Progressive Party's nomination.

The Democratic Party leadership had had its eye on Woodrow Wilson for a long time. He had been mentioned as a potential presidential candidate several years earlier, and although he had been elected to public office for the first time only two years earlier, Wilson received support from important people. Still, his nomination was not

Woodrow Wilson had little political experience when he was elected to the presidency in 1912. Although Wilson was up against two men who had already served as president, Wilson won the election with a majority of the electoral vote.

guaranteed. For a long time, it looked like the Democratic nominee would be James Beauchamp "Champ" Clark, the Speaker of the House of Representatives. At the national Democratic convention, however, Clark did not have the required two-thirds majority of votes to be chosen as the Democratic candidate. Another contender, Congressman

Oscar W. Underwood, decided to bow out of the race, and asked his delegates to vote for Wilson rather than Clark. This turn of events caused Wilson to gain the votes he needed, and Wilson won on the 46th ballot.

In those days, presidential campaigns were very different than they are today. There was no television, so for candidates to get their messages out, they had to rely largely on public rallies and newspaper coverage. Wilson ran for president on what he called his "New Freedom" platform. He promised to strengthen the American economy by breaking up monopolies, which would enable smaller businesses to compete with bigger businesses. He spoke only about domestic issues during his campaign, never about foreign affairs. Although he expressed support for social welfare legislation, most reformers felt that Roosevelt was a better candidate.

At the end, it was a very tightly run race. On Election Day, the American people were far from united. More than 900,000 people voted for the Socialist, Eugene Debs. The Republican Party split, with many members voting for Roosevelt rather than Taft. Taft ended up with 3,484,980 votes. Roosevelt received a half-million more, with 4,119,538 votes. Wilson received two million more than Roosevelt, winning 6,293,454 votes. He did not win what is called the popular vote: Even though he had more votes than Taft, Roosevelt, and Debs individually, their combined votes were greater than Wilson's. Nevertheless, he won the vote in the electoral college, receiving 435 of the 531 votes.

Woodrow Wilson was inaugurated on March 4, 1913. A president with little political experience, Wilson intended to focus on domestic matters and spent his first years pushing through important legislation for the country.

PRESIDENT WILSON

Woodrow Wilson was 55 years old when he was inaugurated as president on March 4, 1913. In less than three years' time, he experienced a meteoric rise, from living as a private citizen who had never held public office to occupying the highest political office in the nation.

Upon Wilson's inauguration, his family moved into the White House. By this time, the Wilson daughters were young women in their mid-twenties. In some ways, Ellen despised having to live in the public eye, but she adapted easily to her new role as First Lady. A gracious woman, she liked to entertain, and people liked to come to the parties she held at the White House.

As he had hoped, Woodrow Wilson was able to concentrate mostly on domestic affairs during his first years as president. As dedicated as ever, he set right to work. He pushed some very important legislation through Congress. He appealed to the American public to pressure their representatives to pass the Underwood Tariff Act, which lowered tariff rates on hundreds of items, creating business opportunities for the "little man." Wilson also fought hard for the Federal Reserve Act, which established 12 Federal Reserve banks that would be run by a board of people appointed by the president. This meant that private bankers lost a great deal of their power to set interest rates and that the government could better control how much money was in circulation at any one time. Wilson also battled for antitrust legislation and labor laws.

> *"It is a fine system where some remote, severe schoolmaster may become president of the United States."*
> — Woodrow Wilson, laughing at himself after he won the presidential election of 1912

POLITICAL UNREST IN MEXICO

Wilson had no experience in foreign affairs when he entered office as president, having only served the public as a state governor. Wilson did not believe in expansionism and publicly stated in 1913 that the United States would "never again seek one additional foot of territory by conquest." Nevertheless, when turmoil broke out in Mexico, he felt he had no choice but to intervene. He did not intend to try to take over Mexico, but he did want a say in who governed that country. Mexican reformer Francisco Madero had removed Mexico's president Porfirio Diaz from office. Within a few short months, Madero was assassinated by supporters of military general Victoriano Huerta. Huerta did not have the entire support of the Mexican people. Worried about American investment in Mexico, among other things, Wilson refused to recognize Huerta as president and sent naval ships to block the port of Vera Cruz so Huerta's army could not receive arms. In April 1914, he sent American soldiers there to fight, vowing, "I am going to teach the South American republics to elect good men."

When Americans killed or wounded 500 Mexican soldiers, Huerta abdicated and Venustiano Carranza, whom Wilson supported, took office. This did not resolve the matter. Soon, Pancho Villa, a bandit chieftain who would win the hearts of the Mexican people, decided to start another revolution and overthrow Carranza.

After Villa's men murdered 16 American engineers in Mexico and then 19 people in New Mexico, Wilson authorized a punitive expedition under the command of General John J. Pershing to go into Mexico and fight Villa.

5

ALLIED HERO:
1914–1921

IN AUGUST 1914, the course of world history changed suddenly when war broke out in Europe. The war was a surprise; Europe had been largely at peace for such a long time that some observers predicted no more wars would erupt there. Under the surface, however, there were serious problems. In the days before the League of Nations and its successor, the United Nations, countries entered into agreements together, forging secret alliances. The world was unaware that Germany, Austria, and Italy had a mutual-defense treaty, which meant that if one country was attacked or decided to go to battle, the others would join in on its side. Great Britain had a secret treaty with France, and France had one with Russia.

Archduke Franz Ferdinand, Austria–Hungary's heir-apparent, walks with his wife Sophie to their car during a visit to Sarajevo on June 28, 1914. Moments later Ferdinand was assassinated by a Serbian nationalist, triggering the start of World War I.

Diplomats had signed these treaties without seriously thinking that their nations would ever be called upon to keep their promises. They did not foresee two developments: The first involved a group of small, rather weak nations in southeastern Europe. After the ancient Ottoman Empire fell apart in the 1870s, the new, independent nations of Serbia, Bulgaria, and Romania emerged. The populations of each of these countries included a large number of members of the Slavic ethnic group. Many Slavs hoped that one day their entire population would live together in one united country. They became "nationalists," advocating one nation for the Slavs. (To this day, they have not succeeded in creating that country, although some continue to fight to do so, as in Bosnia.)

The second development is connected to the first. Both Austria–Hungary and Germany had imperial ambitions. They wanted to grow larger, by taking over their neighbors, if necessary. In 1908, Austria–Hungary annexed Bosnia–Herzogovina, which sat on its southern border. This made the Slavs who lived there angry, and it infuriated many Serbians, who had hoped that that the area would one day be part of the dreamed-of Pan-Slavic country. These emotions would be long lasting and fuel violence.

In June 1914, Archduke Franz Ferdinand, Austria's heir apparent (the expected successor), and his wife paid a state visit to Bosnia. While on what was expected to be an uneventful drive through the streets of Sarajevo, Bosnia's capital, Ferdinand was assassinated by a gunman. An investigation revealed that the killer was a Bosnian who supported the Pan-Slavic cause and had been in com-munication with fellow nationalists in Serbia. Austria delivered an ultimatum to Serbia, which demanded that Serbia allow Austria to enter the country to apprehend the assassins and attack Pan-Slavic nationalism. The ultimatum essentially sought to reduce Serbia's national independence.

Serbia, of course, gave a negative reply, and Austria responded by declaring war on Serbia. Russia started to prepare to fight because it had a secret treaty with Serbia. Germany, Austria's ally, declared war on Russia and France. Great Britain, with its links to France, joined in as well. Almost all of Europe was divided in the war between the Allies (which included Great Britain, France, Italy, and Russia) and the Central Powers (which included Germany, Austria–Hungary, Turkey, and Bulgaria).

When the news crossed the Atlantic Ocean, Wilson proclaimed the United States to be neutral in the conflict. He vowed that the United States would not take sides. Nevertheless, it soon became clear that the war was going to disrupt American life. The United States did a lot of trade with Europe in general, and particularly with Great Britain. Rich Americans had also been in the habit of going to Europe for what was called the Grand Tour, a trip around continental Europe that could last for months.

PERSONAL TRAGEDY

Just as Wilson began to sort out what war would mean to American trade and tourists, he faced a crisis in his personal life. Ellen, his wife of 29 years, had become ill. In March, she had fallen, which aggravated an old kidney ailment. She got out of bed in time for their daughter Eleanor's wedding in May, but from that point on, her health worsened. Doctors diagnosed her as suffering from Bright's disease (a disease that affects the kidneys). Wilson denied to himself the seriousness of Ellen's situation for a long time but finally admitted that she was terminally ill. He spent a great deal of the summer at her bedside. When she died on August 6, some historians believe Wilson suffered a long bout of depression.

Despite his grief, Wilson had to keep working. Important events occurred during this period of his presidency. The Panama Canal, the building of which had been sponsored in large part by the American government, opened to commercial shipping traffic. The Federal Trade Commission, which he had worked very hard for, was established, and Congress passed the Clayton Antitrust Act, also according to Wilson's wishes. In the new year he would have trouble getting Congress to do much that he wanted because in 1914 Americans had elected more Republicans than Democrats, shifting the balance of power in Congress from being mostly Democratic (and therefore favoring Wilson and his Democratic policies) to mostly Republican (and therefore more opposed to Wilson and his Democratic policies).

THE WAR AFFECTS AMERICANS

For a time, in terms of foreign affairs, Wilson seemed to remain most deeply concerned about developments in Latin America in general and Mexico in particular. Matters in Europe, though, would take up more and more of his time. When the war first began, Great Britain interfered with U.S. shipping first by stopping American merchant ships bound for Germany (to look for weapons) and then

Men carry the body of one the 128 Americans killed when Germany sank the British ship *Lusitania* in May 1915. Although Wilson first believed that the United States should remain neutral during the war, Germany's aggressive actions made it increasingly difficult for both the president and the nation to ignore the war raging in Europe.

by mining the North Sea and blockading German ports. Wilson protested their actions but to no avail.

Early the next year, he became much more concerned about what he saw as Germany's violation of U.S. rights. Germany's navy included U-boats, which are submarines equipped with torpedoes. In February of 1915, Germany declared the seas around Great Britain a war zone and warned other nations not to sail ships there.

Wilson demanded "strict accountability," warning Germany that if its submarines fired on any ships carrying Americans, he would hold the Germans responsible for lost American lives. A few Americans did in fact die when U-boats torpedoed British ships and an American tanker.

Germany then went further, paying for an advertisement placed in American newspapers on May 1 that warned American travelers not to board British or French ships. On May 7, a U-boat downed a British luxury liner, the *Lusitania*. Of the more than 1,000 passengers who died, 128 were American.

The nation was divided over the proper course to follow. Many Americans had suddenly begun to view Germany as the enemy. They demanded that the United States prepare to go to war. The ever-vocal Theodore Roosevelt publicly criticized Wilson as a coward. By the fall of 1915, Wilson himself had begun to question the wisdom of neutrality and made plans for a military buildup.

On the other hand, there was another very large group of Americans that clamored to stay out of war. It included German Americans, pacifists, and progressives who warned that the United States could not both fight in the war and continue its movement toward reform.

Even as this debate took place, Wilson experienced a new change in his personal life. He started to date a widow named Edith Galt, who lived in Washington, D.C. They married in December 1915.

THE ELECTION OF 1916

Wilson sought re-election in 1916. The Democratic Party used "He has kept us out of war" as its slogan. The Republican candidate, Charles Evan Hughes, never took a final stand on American involvement in the war: At times, Hughes criticized Wilson for war-mongering, but at other times he criticized Wilson for being a coward.

When the election took place in November, the results were too close to call. Some newspapers declared Hughes the winner, but that was a mistake. In reality, Wilson edged him out a narrow margin, receiving nine million votes as opposed to Hughes' eight and a half-million. Despite the small victory, the country rallied behind Wilson.

In 1916, Germany agreed to restrict its submarine warfare, accepting American demands that it stop sinking passenger liners and neutral countries' cargo ships. In January of 1917, however, Germany resumed using its U-boats as it had earlier and formally announced the decision on January 31. Wilson broke diplomatic relations with Germany on February 3. On February 24, the president learned that British spies had intercepted what is now known as the Zimmermann Telegram. Sent by the German foreign secretary to the German ambassador to Mexico, the telegram proposed that in the case that the United States declared war on Germany, the ambassador should try to forge an alliance among Germany, Japan, and Mexico. He told the ambassador to promise Mexican officials that if they emerged victorious, Germany would force the United States to give Texas, New Mexico, and Arizona back to Mexico. This occurred at the very end of Wilson's first term.

Wilson's second term began with his inauguration on March 5, 1917. Just a few days later, Germans sank three American merchant ships. Wilson moved quickly, asking Congress to declare war on Germany on April 2, 1917. A bitter debate followed, but in the end Congress did as he asked.

America then mobilized for war, moving very quickly to build up its military. As the nation's young men volunteered to fight by the thousands and were sent for military training and then overseas, life changed in the United States. Families were torn apart. The government expanded dramatically, creating new departments and instituting new rules designed to increase security.

> *"The four years which have elapsed since last I stood in this place have been crowded with counsel and action of the most vital interest and consequence. Perhaps no equal period in our history has been so fruitful of important reforms in our economic and industrial life or so full of significant changes in the spirit and purpose of our political action. We have sought very thoughtfully to set our house in order, correct the grosser errors and abuses of our industrial life, liberate and quicken the processes of our national genius and energy, and lift our politics to a broader view of the people's essential interests."*
>
> — Woodrow Wilson, in his Second Inaugural Address, March 5, 1917

Despite its late entry, the United States played an extremely important part in World War I. Its massive infusion of men and arms created a great advantage for the Allies and turned the tide of the war in their favor. This victory, however, came at a great price. Much of World War I was fought in trenches. Soldiers had to hunker for days, even weeks, in pits that were often cold and muddy. It could take days and weeks for armies to advance just a small distance. There was some hand-to-hand fighting, but many deaths were caused by artillery (bombs and cannons) and poison gas. British political leaders later described trench warfare as "the most gigantic, tenacious, grim, futile, and bloody fight every waged in the history of war."

THE FOURTEEN POINTS

Wilson stressed to America that its boys were fighting this terrible battle for what he described as a new democratic world order. Early on, he became concerned about the nature of the peace that would follow the end of the war. On January 8, 1918, he went before Congress to deliver what is commonly called his Fourteen Points speech, in which he listed what he considered essential to bringing about a just and lasting peace. As the final point of his speech, he called for a new world order to be based on a "general association of nations." When the Allies read his Fourteen Points, they agreed to follow most of his plan. England would not agree to Wilson's second point, which called for the freedom of the seas, and France demanded

(continued on page 68)

Wilson's Fourteen Points

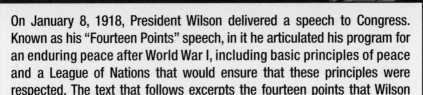

On January 8, 1918, President Wilson delivered a speech to Congress. Known as his "Fourteen Points" speech, in it he articulated his program for an enduring peace after World War I, including basic principles of peace and a League of Nations that would ensure that these principles were respected. The text that follows excerpts the fourteen points that Wilson called for in his speech.

1. Open covenants of peace, openly arrived at, after which there shall be no private international understandings of any kind but diplomacy shall proceed always frankly and in the public view.

2. Absolute freedom of navigation upon the seas, outside territorial waters, alike in peace and in war, except as the seas may be closed in whole or in part by international action for the enforcement of international covenants.

3. The removal, so far as possible, of all economic barriers and the establishment of an equality of trade conditions among all the nations consenting to the peace and associating themselves for its maintenance.

4. Adequate guarantees given and taken that national armaments will be reduced to the lowest point consistent with domestic safety.

5. A free, open-minded, and absolutely impartial adjustment of all colonial claims, based upon a strict observance of the principle that in determining all such questions of sovereignty the interests of the populations concerned must have equal weight with the equitable claims of the government whose title is to be determined.

6. The evacuation of all Russian territory and such a settlement of all questions affecting Russia as will secure the best and freest cooperation of the other nations of the world in obtaining for her an unhampered and unembarrassed opportunity for the independent determination of her own political development and national policy and assure her of a sincere welcome into the society of free nations under institutions of her own choosing; and, more than a welcome, assistance also of every kind that she may need and may herself desire. The treatment accorded Russia by her sister nations in the months to come will be the acid test of their good will, of their comprehension of her needs as distinguished from their own interests, and of their intelligent and unselfish sympathy.

7. Belgium, the whole world will agree, must be evacuated and restored, without any attempt to limit the sovereignty which she enjoys in common

with all other free nations. No other single act will serve as this will serve to restore confidence among the nations in the laws which they have themselves set and determined for the government of their relations with one another. Without this healing act the whole structure and validity of international law is forever impaired.

8. All French territory should be freed and the invaded portions restored, and the wrong done to France by Prussia in 1871 in the matter of Alsace-Lorraine, which has unsettled the peace of the world for nearly fifty years, should be righted, in order that peace may once more be made secure in the interest of all.

9. A readjustment of the frontiers of Italy should be effected along clearly recognizable lines of nationality.

10. The peoples of Austria–Hungary, whose place among the nations we wish to see safeguarded and assured, should be accorded the freest opportunity of autonomous development.

11. Rumania, Serbia, and Montenegro should be evacuated; occupied territories restored; Serbia accorded free and secure access to the sea; and the relations of the several Balkan states to one another determined by friendly counsel along historically established lines of allegiance and nationality; and international guarantees of the political and economic independence and territorial integrity of the several Balkan states should be entered into.

12. The Turkish portions of the present Ottoman Empire should be assured a secure sovereignty, but the other nationalities which are now under Turkish rule should be assured an undoubted security of life and an absolutely unmolested opportunity of an autonomous development, and the Dardanelles should be permanently opened as a free passage to the ships and commerce of all nations under international guarantees.

13. An independent Polish state should be erected which should include the territories inhabited by indisputably Polish populations, which should be assured a free and secure access to the sea, and whose political and economic independence and territorial integrity should be guaranteed by international covenant.

14. A general association of nations must be formed under specific covenants for the purpose of affording mutual guarantees of political independence and territorial integrity to great and small states alike.

(continued from page 65)

that Germany be forced to pay reparations (fines) to the help the countries whose land and industries had been destroyed by the war rebuild.

In October 1918, Wilson contributed to the end of the war when he exchanged peace notes with Germany and Austria–Hungary. The war finally ended in November, and the Allies celebrated Armistice Day. Great Britain, France, Russia, and the United States had defeated Germany and Austria–Hungary. A peace conference, which would later come to be known as the Paris Peace Conference, was called to write a treaty that would officially end the war and ensure a long-lasting peace in Europe. Against the wishes of the Senate, Wilson decided to attend. He wanted a chance to talk in person to Europe's leaders about the principles he strongly believed in. He stated up front that he would insist that the treaty include arrangements to establish the League of Nations, which Wilson had envisioned as an international alliance, which much like the United Nations today, would work to ensure peace in the world.

Wilson promised to be absent from the United States for as short a time as possible. (In the early twentieth century, before airplanes could fly across the oceans, it was necessary to sail from one continent to the other, meaning that he would be gone for at least two months). The senators feared that he would neglect what they considered to be the country's priorities—business at home, like the economy. Many congressmen resented the fact that he had not consulted with them as to what actions he should take in Paris.

Edith accompanied Wilson on this trip, a trip that made him the first president to visit Europe while in office. The Wilsons made the voyage across the Atlantic Ocean on a navy ship. For recreation, they walked on deck and went below to listen to the crew sing. The French were eager to welcome Wilson: it was his leadership that guided the United States during the war and contributed to the Allied victory. As the ship entered the harbor of Brest, France,

> *"I have won a sweet companion who will soon make me forget the intolerable loneliness and isolation of the weary months since this terrible war began."*
> — Woodrow Wilson, about his marriage to Edith Galt in 1915

on December 13, 1918, war vessels shot their cannons in welcoming salutes. Wilson, standing at the railing, waved to all he could see. A small boat carried the president to the quay, where officials had gathered to greet him formally. The streets all around were crowded with people, including many children who waved American flags. Wilson was especially cheered when he saw a banner congratulating him on founding the League of Nations, even though he had yet to do so.

From Brest, the president, Edith, and his aides traveled to Paris. There, soldiers lined the avenues through which his car passed. Behind the soldiers stood thousands and thousands of people, some yelling greetings and others weeping for joy. Banners in his honor hung from the city's ancient buildings.

Some of Wilson's time was spent visiting American soldiers who remained in France, recovering in hospitals from war wounds. He also met with France's president, Georges Clemenceau. The British envoys were late arriving, so, eager to meet its representatives, Wilson took a short side trip to England, where he met the king and the prime minister, Lloyd George.

On December 31, Wilson returned to the Continent and headed for Italy, where he was likewise treated as a hero. Arriving in France, he felt extremely confident and optimistic. In the days that followed, though, his mood began to change. Even before the conference began, he was given cause to distrust both France and England. First, he found out that the French had deliberately not sent aid to one war-ravaged area in France until he had been to see it. They hoped that if Wilson saw the terrible condition of the region, he would be more likely to support the French demand that Germany pay reparations for the damage France had suffered because of the war. Then Wilson learned that Lloyd George was telling other members of the British delegation that Americans did not fully support Wilson and that Congress might not honor the promises Wilson made at the Paris Peace Conference.

His mood continued to deteriorate by the time all the delegates gathered at Versailles on January 12, 1919. Wilson had hoped that just four men, known as the "Big Four"—the political leaders of France, Britain, and Italy, and himself—would sit down to discuss the terms of the treaty. (Russia could not participate because revolution had broken out there and the country was in disarray; Germany would have no say, because it had

Wilson had high hopes for the Paris Peace Conference, where he proposed the League of Nations. The conference included the major leaders of the Allies: (from left to right) David Lloyd George of Great Britain, Vittorio Orlando of Italy, Georges Clemenceau of France, and Woodrow Wilson.

been defeated.) Instead of only four people gathering to talk about the terms to be offered to Germany, however, the conference room was filled with 22 people, including secretaries, interpreters, and other "experts."

Wilson was happy when, early on, the delegates passed resolutions favoring the creation of the League of Nations, but he had to yield on other points that he felt strongly about. Ultimately, he thought the final treaty punished Germany far too harshly. Not only was Germany disarmed and stripped of some of its wealthiest colonies, but it was also forced to accept blame for starting the war and to agree to pay huge reparations to France and Great Britain. Wilson was later able to persuade the other delegates to promise that the former German colonies would not always belong to the victors but would one day become independent and create two new nations, Czechoslovakia (which became the separate countries of the Czech Republic and Slovakia in 1993) and Yugoslavia (which became the separate countries of Serbia and Montenegro in 2003).

In the final analysis, Wilson largely failed to achieve

The Treaty of Versailles

At the Paris Peace Conference beginning January 18, 1919, the leaders of the Allies met at the Palace of Versailles to agree on an official peace settlement. The four leaders of the major Allied powers, known as the "Big Four," were France's Georges Clemenceau, Great Britain's David Lloyd George, Italy's Vittorio Orlando, and Woodrow Wilson. Each leader had his own set of goals for the peace agreement. Although Wilson attended the peace conference, the United States did not sign the Treaty of Versailles with the other Allied powers on June 28, 1919; instead the United States signed its own treaty with Germany, the Treaty of Berlin, on July 2, 1921.

The major results of the Treaty of Versailles were:

Germany had to:

- Reduce its army to 100,000 men and was not allowed to have a draft

- Reduce its navy to six warships and could not have any submarines

- Destroy all of its airforce

- Hand over land to Belgium, France, Denmark, and Poland

- Give up its colonies

the goals that he meant to accomplish. Historians have concluded that although he excelled at rhetoric (persuasive speech) and oratory (public speaking), he lacked the negotiation skills necessary to deal with the other powerful individuals at the Paris Peace Conference.

THE LEAGUE OF NATIONS

Before Wilson left Europe to return to the United States, a League Commission met. He helped draw up the League of

- Pay reparations to the Allies for all of the damage caused by the war

- Refrain from positioning soldiers or military equipment within 30 miles of the east bank of the Rhine river

- Accept all blame for the war

- Accept a new government by the Allies to prevent the country from being taken over by a dictatorship

Italy:

- Was given land in the areas of Istria and the South Tirol

Other:

- Poland, Lithuania, Latvia, Estonia and Finland were formed from land lost by Russia

- Czechoslovakia (today the separate countries of the Czech Republic and Slovakia) and Hungary were formed out of the Austro-Hungarian Empire

- The Adriatic Coast was incorporated into a new country called Yugoslavia (today the two separate countries of Serbia and Montenegro)

Nations' covenant or constitution. The covenant contained articles pledging that its members would arbitrate disagreements between countries that seemed likely to lead to war. Members also promised not to go to war with other nations that abided by the terms of the covenant. The covenant called for small powers as well as large powers to have a say, which Wilson wanted. He would later be disappointed when large powers in the league turned out to have more power than the small nations.

> "The world must be made safe for democracy. Its peace must be planted upon the tested foundations of political liberty. We have no selfish ends to serve. We desire no conquest, no dominion. . . . We are but one of the champions of the rights of mankind. We shall be satisfied when those rights have been made as secure as the faith and the freedom of nations can make them."
> — Woodrow Wilson, War Message to Congress, April 2, 1917

WILSON RETURNS HOME

On February 15, 1919 the Wilsons headed home. While he had been gone, important events had taken place back at home. On January 26, 1919 the Eighteenth Amendment to the Constitution had been ratified, making the manufacture, sale, or transportation of liquor illegal in the United States. The country was now "dry."

Some problems had arisen because of his absence, just as his critics had predicted. When his train arrived in Washington, D.C., on February 24, Wilson worried for a time because crowds did not turn out to meet him. He was cheered when he learned that there had been throngs of citizens waiting to greet him, but because his train had been so late, they finally sadly dispersed.

Back at the White House, he prepared for his next fight: persuading the Senate to ratify the Versailles Treaty. At first he did not expect this to be very hard. Many Americans clearly had high hopes for the League of Nations. Over time, though, Wilson realized that he was going to have much more trouble than he had anticipated.

6

GLOBAL
LEGACY

WHEN WOODROW WILSON arrived home from Europe in
February of 1919, he was just two weeks short of being halfway
through his second term as president. Campaigning for the next
presidential elections would begin in about a year.

PROBLEMS AT HOME

In terms of domestic politics, debate had begun on the Nineteenth
Amendment, which would give women the right to vote. Historians
see this as one of the great successes of the progressive movement.
Yet even as one reform goal was met, the positive feeling inspired
by the movement began to die. During the war's aftermath,

A strike leader speaks to a crowd of workers in Gary, Indiana, in 1919. Social unrest became a problem following the end of World War I. Wilson had to deal with strikes, riots, and the fear of Communism while still trying to persuade the U.S. Senate to ratify the Treaty of Versailles.

"conformism and fear of radicalism set in," in the words of one historian. There was terrible racial violence in 1919.

That same year, people displayed a great fear of "Bolshevism," or Communism. Strikers were suddenly accused of being Communists, dangerous dissenters, and agitators. Politicians got caught up in the fray. First, the House of Representatives refused to recognize a Socialist who had been elected and would not permit him to enter Congress. At least one state legislature expelled its Socialist members. The Justice Department started to arrest hundreds of people because they were suspected of being Communists, and the government deported Russian aliens.

Woodrow Wilson paid little attention to these developments; almost all of his energy went into efforts he made for the League of Nations. He wanted to persuade the Senate to ratify the Treaty of Versailles, but the Senate included some new faces and some very vocal critics. Senator William E. Borah considered the treaty unacceptable as long as it included any clause indicating that the United States would join the League of Nations. Others such as Senator Henry Cabot Lodge said they could support a league but not as it stood now. Wilson, completely unwilling to compromise, prepared to fight his opponents.

THE BEGINNING OF THE END

In March, Wilson went on a second trip to Europe. By this time, he was ill and looked like an old man. He also no longer enjoyed the popularity he had just after the war. The French were angry with him because they thought they would not receive their reparations. England wanted the United States to promise not to build up a strong navy. Wilson spent weeks working on final negotiations concerning the treaty and the Covenant of the League of Nations.

Back home, at the end of the spring, he called Congress into a special session to resolve labor problems. The Treaty of Versailles was finally shown to the Germans and signed by all parties on June 28, 1919. The U.S. Senate, though, could not agree to ratify the treaty. In August, Wilson's attention was diverted when he tried to settle a railway strike. In September, he decided to appeal directly to the American public to push their senators to ratify the Treaty of Versailles. He started out on a whistle-stop campaign on September 3, boarding a special train that would carry him west, making stop after stop so that he could speak in person to the public. He traveled more than 9,000 miles, delivering 37 speeches in 22 days.

For a time, he seemed to be enjoying the trip and experiencing success—the crowds that turned out to meet him were very friendly. Then, on the evening of September 25, he collapsed from exhaustion. His aides made the decision that he could do no more and had the train head back to Washington. On October 2, he had a stroke. By October 4, he was described as having suffered a complete physical breakdown. From this point on, he rarely left his bed and his wheelchair.

On November 19, 1919, the Senate voted to reject the Treaty of Versailles. On January 13, 1920, the League of Nations held its first meeting. The United States never joined. In January, people suggested that Wilson resign, but he refused. For a time, Wilson even talked of running for election to a third term, but he received no support. The Democratic Party nominated someone else. Wilson had almost no influence on the election, which resulted in the inauguration of Republican Warren G. Harding.

Wilson did almost nothing during the months that he was the lame duck president. His cabinet members took care of the business of the executive branch of the government, but Edith took over much of the work that her husband had done—which led to some historians calling her the United

PRESIDENT WILSON'S LEGACY

Woodrow Wilson International Center for Scholars

Woodrow Wilson has the distinction of being the only U.S. president with a Ph.D. Often called the "schoolmaster in politics," referring to his days as a professor and university president, Wilson was an idealist and an intellectual. He wrote many books in which he discussed public policy and government. One of these books includes his proposal for the idea of an international organization that would maintain world peace. Wilson would return to this idea after World War I and develop it into the League of Nations. Though the league would disband after a few years, Presidents Franklin Delano Roosevelt and Harry S. Truman would revisit the idea at the end of World War II and work to establish the United Nations, which continues to promote international peace to this day.

Although the United States never did ratify the Treaty of Versailles and join the League of Nations, the global community recognized the incredible effort and passion Wilson applied to make the league possible and awarded him the Nobel Peace Prize. Over time, however, the United States has also come to realize the magnitude of Wilson's contributions as an intellectual and policy maker. The U.S. Congress established the Woodrow Wilson International Center for Scholars in 1968 as a memorial to his work. While most great American presidents are given tributes in statues of stone, President Wilson's

States' first female president. After Harding was sworn in, Wilson and his wife continued to live in Washington, D.C., as private citizens. Wilson stayed out of the public eye.

On February 3, 1924, only three years after he left office, Woodrow Wilson died. He was buried in state in Washington, D.C. Although Americans reacted to the news with grief, opinions were still divided over the sort of

memorial is a living tribute that carries on in his spirit, furthering intellectual discussions of public policy and endeavoring to use these intellectual discussions to engender change.

The Woodrow Wilson International Center for Scholars is a nonpartisan institution located in Washington, D.C. The goal of the center is to provide a forum in which ideas and policy can connect. The center also encourages research, study, discussion and the collaboration between scholars and policy makers. Bringing together individuals from the worlds of scholarship, policy, and business, the center supports research in a variety of areas from the humanities and social sciences, particularly history, political science, and international relations.

The center strives to reach as many people as possible and has pursued numerous avenues to communicate with the public, from radio and television programs, its *Wilson Quarterly* magazine, and numerous books published by its own press to websites, newsletters, and open discussions.

The Woodrow Wilson International Center for Scholars is a far more appropriate memorial for a man whose passion and determination changed the world than a stone monument. Although Wilson was not fully appreciated in his time, his remarkable legacy is recognized today and continues in the center established in his honor.

president he had been. With time, however, more and more people came to recognize the value of his vision. Later presidents drew on precedents he had set. Franklin Delano Roosevelt, in particular, came to believe that Woodrow Wilson had been absolutely right in believing that the

PRESIDENT WILSON'S LEGACY

The President and the American Public

Asked about Woodrow Wilson's legacy, historian David M. Kennedy said that one of the things that was special about Wilson was his relationship with the American public. Just 11 days after his first inauguration, Wilson made history when he became the first president to hold an open press conference. Earlier presidents invited only a few of their favorite journalists at a time to speak to them, but Wilson threw open the doors and invited anyone who reported White House news to come hear him speak and ask him questions. Thus write-ups of what he had to say appeared in a greater number and a greater variety of magazines and newspapers, allowing him to reach a larger audience.

Throughout his political career, Wilson also maintained a huge correspondence, reading letters from and writing to ordinary Americans. Toward the end of his presidency, he made his most valiant attempt to communicate with the American people when he launched his whistle-stop campaign. His goal was to meet voters and persuade them to tell their representatives to vote for his beloved League of Nations. Kennedy later summed up what Wilson did by saying, "He's one of the people early in this century who understands number one, that the president as he put it himself is free to be as big a man as he can be. That he's not merely the servant of the legislature. He understands the power of the president to deal directly with the people." Other very strong presidents of the twentieth century, including Franklin Roosevelt and John F. Kennedy, have followed in Wilson's footsteps, seeking to speak directly to the public in times of crisis or change.

Mourners bow their heads in respect outside the home of Woodrow Wilson in Washington, D.C. after his death in 1924. At the time of his death, opinion over Wilson's presidency was still divided. Today, Wilson is recognized for his brilliant vision and unfailing determination to establish a just and lasting peace in the world after World War I.

nations of the world must cooperate if peace were to reign.

Wilson's beloved League of Nations eventually died (it finally disbanded in 1939), but it was replaced by another association, the United Nations, which operates under principles he outlined. As the first years of the twenty-first century have already demonstrated, the United Nations is an organization so influential that its role in world affairs is a topic of constant debate. Today, scholars recognize Woodrow Wilson as one of the most influential U.S. presidents. Although his political career was not without setbacks, in his efforts to establish long-lasting peace, Wilson not only impacted the United States but the entire world.

THE PRESIDENTS
OF THE
UNITED STATES

George Washington
1789–1797

John Adams
1797–1801

Thomas Jefferson
1801–1809

James Madison
1809–1817

James Monroe
1817–1825

John Quincy Adams
1825–1829

Andrew Jackson
1829–1837

Martin Van Buren
1837–1841

William Henry
Harrison
1841

John Tyler
1841–1845

James Polk
1845–1849

Zachary Taylor
1849–1850

Millard Filmore
1850–1853

Franklin Pierce
1853–1857

James Buchanan
1857–1861

Abraham Lincoln
1861–1865

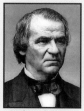

Andrew Johnson
1865–1869

Ulysses S. Grant
1869–1877

Rutherford B. Hayes
1877–1881

James Garfield
1881

Chester Arthur
1881–1885

Grover Cleveland
1885–1889

Benjamin Harrison
1889–1893

Grover Cleveland
1893-1897

William McKinley
1897–1901

Theodore Roosevelt
1901–1909

William H. Taft
1909–1913

Woodrow Wilson
1913–1921

Warren Harding
1921–1923

Calvin Coolidge
1923–1929

Herbert Hoover
1929–1933

Franklin D. Roosevelt 1933–1945

Harry S. Truman
1945–1953

Dwight Eisenhower
1953–1961

John F. Kennedy
1961–1963

Lyndon Johnson
1963–1969

Richard Nixon
1969–1974

Gerald Ford
1974–1977

Jimmy Carter
1977–1981

Ronald Reagan
1981–1989

George H.W. Bush
1989–1993

William J. Clinton
1993–2001

George W. Bush
2001–

Note: Dates indicate years of presidential service.
Source: www.whitehouse.gov

PRESIDENTIAL FACT FILE

THE CONSTITUTION

Article II of the Constitution of the United States outlines several require-
ments for the president of the United States, including:

★ **Age:** The president must be at least 35 years old.

★ **Citizenship:** The president must be a U.S. citizen.

★ **Residency:** The president must have lived in the United States for
at least 14 years.

★ **Oath of Office:** On his inauguration, the president takes this oath:
"I do solemnly swear (or affirm) that I will faithfully execute
the office of President of the United States, and will to the best
of my ability, preserve, protect and defend the Constitution of
the United States."

★ **Term:** A presidential term lasts four years.

PRESIDENTIAL POWERS

The president has many distinct powers as outlined in and interpreted
from the Constitution. The president:

★ Submits many proposals to Congress for regulatory, social, and
economic reforms.

★ Appoints federal judges with the Senate's approval.

★ Prepares treaties with foreign nations to be approved by the
Senate.

★ Can veto laws passed by Congress.

★ Acts as commander in chief of the military to oversee military
strategy and actions.

★ Appoints members of the cabinet and many other agencies and
administrations with the Senate's approval.

★ Can declare martial law (control of local governments within
the country) in times of national crisis.

Presidential Fact File

TRADITION

Many parts of the presidency developed out of tradition. The traditions listed below are but a few that are associated with the U.S. presidency.

★ After taking his oath of office, George Washington added, "So help me God." Numerous presidents since Washington have also added this phrase to their oath.

★ Originally, the Constitution limited the term of the presidency to four years, but did not limit the number of terms a president could serve. Presidents, following the precedent set by George Washington, traditionally served only two terms. After Franklin Roosevelt was elected to four terms, however, Congress amended the Constitution to restrict presidents to only two.

★ James Monroe was the first president to have his inauguration outside the Capitol. From his inauguration in 1817 to Jimmy Carter's inauguration in 1977, it was held on the Capitol's east portico. Ronald Reagan broke from this tradition in 1981 when he was inaugurated on the west portico to face his home state, California. Since 1981, all presidential inaugurations have been held on the west portico of the Capitol.

★ Not all presidential traditions are serious, however. One of the more fun activities connected with the presidency began when President William Howard Taft ceremoniously threw out the first pitch of the new baseball season in 1910.  Presidents since Taft have carried on this tradition, including Woodrow Wilson, who is pictured here as he throws the first pitch of the 1916 season. In more recent years, the president has also opened the All-Star and World Series games.

Presidential Fact File

THE WHITE HOUSE

Although George Washington was involved with the planning of the White House, he never lived there. It has been, however, the official residence of every president beginning with John Adams, the second U.S. president. The

building was completed approximately in 1800, although it has undergone several renovations since then. It was the first public building constructed in Washington, D.C. The White House has 132 rooms, several of which are open to the public. Private rooms include those for administration and the president's personal residence. For an online tour of the White House and other interesting facts, visit the official White House website, *http://www.whitehouse.gov.*

THE PRESIDENTIAL SEAL

A committee began planning the presidential seal in 1777. It was completed in 1782. The seal appears as an official stamp on medals, stationery, and documents, among other items. Originally, the eagle faced right toward the arrows (a symbol of war) that it held in its talons. In 1945, President Truman had the seal altered so that the eagle's head instead faced left toward the olive branch (a symbol of peace), because he believed the president should be prepared for war but always look toward peace.

PRESIDENT WILSON IN PROFILE

PERSONAL

Name: Thomas Woodrow Wilson

Birth date: December 28, 1856

Birth place: Staunton, Virginia

Father: Joseph Ruggles Wilson

Mother: Jessie Janet Woodrow

Wife: Ellen Axson (d.1914); Edith Galt

Children: Margaret, Jessie, and Eleanor

Death date: February 3, 1924

Death place: Washington, D.C.

POLITICAL

Years in office: 1913–1921

Vice president: Thomas R. Marshall

Occupations before presidency: Lawyer, university professor, governor

Political party: Democrat

Major achievements of presidency: Leading nation during World War I, establishing League of Nations

Nickname: Schoolmaster in Politics

Presidential library:

The Woodrow Wilson Presidential Library
18-24 North Coalter Street (P.O. Box 24)
Staunton, Virginia 24402-0024
540-885-0897
http://www.woodrowwilson.org

Tributes:

Woodrow Wilson House
(Washington, D.C.; *http://www.woodrowwilsonhouse.org*)

Woodrow Wilson International Center for Scholars
(Washington, D.C.; *http:// wwics.si.edu*)

CHRONOLOGY

1856   Thomas Woodrow Wilson is born on December 28.

1860   The Wilson family moves from Staunton, Virginia, to Augusta, Georgia.

1861   The Civil War begins.

1867   Tommy Wilson starts private school.

1870   The Wilson family moves to Columbia, South Carolina.

1873   Davidson College accepts Tommy Wilson as a student. He will not finish his second year there.

1875   Enrolls in the College of New Jersey.

1879   Starts law school.

1883   Begins work toward a doctorate degree at Johns Hopkins University.

1885   Marries Ellen Axson, has his first book published, and becomes a college professor.

1888   Accepts a new professorship at Wesleyan.

1890   Returns to his alma mater, the College of New Jersey, to teach.

1902   Becomes president of Princeton University, formerly the College of New Jersey.

1910   Wins election as governor of New Jersey.

1912   Successfully campaigns for the presidency.

1914   American soldiers start a "punitive campaign" in Mexico. World War I begins, but the United States stays out of it.

1916   Wilson wins election to a second term as president.

1917   On April 2, Wilson asks Congress to declare war on Germany, bringing the United States into World War I on the side of Great Britain, France, and Russia.

1918   First speaks of the League of Nations in the Fourteen Points speech delivered to Congress.

CHRONOLOGY

1919 Attends the peace conference in Europe to work out details of Germany's surrender. He suffers a stroke while campaigning to persuade Americans to push senators to ratify the Versailles Treaty.

1920 Wins the Nobel Peace Prize for 1919. He cannot attend the ceremony in Oslo, Norway, because he is ill.

1924 Woodrow Wilson dies at his home in Washington, D.C.

Bibliography

Anderson, David D. *Woodrow Wilson.* Boston: Twayne Publishers, 1978.

Auchincloss, Louis. *Woodrow Wilson: A Penguin Life.* New York: Viking Press, 2000.

Baker, Ray Stannard. *Woodrow Wilson, Life and Letters.* New York: Doubleday, Doran & Co. 1927–1939.

Boyer, Paul S., et al. *The Enduring Vision: A History of the American People* Vol. 2. Lexington, Mass.: D.C. Heath and Company, 1993.

Braeman, John, ed. *Wilson.* Englewood Cliffs, N.J.: Prentice-Hall, Inc., 1972.

Hakim, Joy. *Freedom! A History of US.* New York: Oxford University Press, 2002.

Knock, Thomas. *To End All Wars: Woodrow Wilson and the Quest for a New World Order.* Princeton, N.J.: Princeton University Press, 1995.

Kuhnhardt Jr., Philip B., et al. *The American President.* New York: Riverhead Books, 1999.

Smith, Gene. *When the Cheering Stopped.* New York: William Morrow and Company, 1964.

Walworth, Arthur. *Woodrow Wilson.* Boston: Houghton Mifflin, 1965.

WEBSITES

Nobel e-Museum: Woodrow Wilson's Acceptance Speech
http://www.nobel.se/peace/laureates/1919/wilson-acceptance.html

PBS: Wilson—A Portrait
http://www.pbs.org/wgbh/amex/wilson/portrait/wp_wilson.html

President Woodrow Wilson's War Message
http://www.lib.byu.edu/~rdh/wwi/1917/wilswarm.html

Princeton in the Nation's Service
http://etc.princeton.edu/CampusWWW/Companion/
princeton_in_nations_service.html

Woodrow Wilson's Fourteen Points Speech
http://usinfo.state.gov/usa/infousa/facts/democrac/51.htm

Hakim, Joy. *A History of US, an Age of Extremes, 1870–1917.* New York: Oxford University Press, 1994.

Hakim, Joy. *A History of US, War, Peace, and All That Jazz, 1917–1929.* New York: Oxford University Press, 1994.

Hakim, Joy. *A History of US, War, Terrible War, 1860–1865.* New York: Oxford University Press, 1994.

Rogers, James T. *Woodrow Wilson: Visionary for Peace.* New York: Facts on File, 1997.

WEBSITES

The Avalon Project at Yale Law School: The Covenant of the League of Nations
http://www.yale.edu/lawweb/avalon/leagcov.htm

The Governors of New Jersey 1664–1974: Biographical Essays
http://www.njstatelib.org/cyberdesk/digidox/digidox6.htm

Princeton University
http://www.princeton.edu

Woodrow Wilson Boyhood Historic Home
http://www.historiccolumbia.org/houses/woodrow.htm

The Woodrow Wilson International Center for Scholars
http://www.wwics.si.edu

The Woodrow Wilson Presidential Library
http://www.woodrowwilson.org/

INDEX

Adams, John
  as U.S. president,
    88
  and the revolution
    against the British,
    7
Addams, Jane, 46
American Civil War,
  19, 21–24, 90
  and the Confederacy,
    21–24
  reconstruction of the
    south, 24–25
  and slavery, 20, 25
American Revolution,
  7
Atlanta, Georgia, 31
Augusta, Georgia, 19,
  21–23, 90
Austria-Hungary, 56
  and World War I, 13,
    57–59, 68

Berlin, Treaty of, 72
Bismarck, Otto von,
  29
Borah, William E.,
  78
Bosnia, 58
Bryn Mawr College,
  33–34
Bulgaria
  and World War I,
    57, 59

"Cabinet Government
  in the United States"
  published college
  thesis, 29
Carnegie, Andrew,
  45
Carranza, Venustiano,
  55

Carter, Jimmy
  as U.S. president,
    87
Chicago Tribune,
  19
Chicago's World Fair
  Wilson's speech at,
    39
Clark, James
  Beauchamp "Champ"
  and the election of
    1912, 51–52
Clayton Antitrust Act,
  60
Clemenceau, Georges,
  President of France
  and the Paris Peace
    Conference, 70–
    72
Cleveland, Grover,
  41
College of New Jersey.
  See Princeton
  University
Columbia, South
  Carolina, 26, 28,
  90
Communism, 77–78
*Congressional Govern-
  ment,* 33
Cronkite, Walter
  foreword, 6–9
Czechoslovakia, 72

Davidson College,
  27–28, 90
Davis, Jefferson
  as president of
    the Confederacy,
    23
Debs, Eugene
  and the election of
    1912, 52

Democratic Party,
  12–13, 41, 47–51,
  60, 63, 65, 79, 89
Diaz, Porfirio, 55
Division and Reunion,
  40

Edison, Thomas, 44
Election of 1912
  candidates of, 49–52
Election of 1916
  candidates of, 63
England, 29, 56, 65,
  78
  and the American
    Revolution, 7
  and the Paris Peace
    Conference, 70–73
  Parliament system
    of, 26
  and World War I, 13,
    15–16, 59–62, 68,
    90
Ethiopia
  Italy's attack on, 16

Federal Reserve Act,
  54
Federal Trade Com-
  mission, 60
Ferdinand, Franz,
  Archduke of Austria-
  Hungary
  assassination of,
    57–58
Fourteen Points
  program, 10, 65–67
France, 56, 78
  and the Paris Peace
    Conference, 70–73
  and World War I,
    13–16, 59, 65, 68,
    90

INDEX

Gary, Indiana, 77
George, David Lloyd,
  Prime Minister of
  England
  and the Paris Peace
    Conference, 70–
    72
Germany, 29, 56, 58,
  70–72, 79
  surrender of, 91
  U-boats 0f, 61–62
  and World War I,
    13–16, 59–64, 66,
    90
  and World War II,
    17
Grant, Ulysses S., 24

Harding, Warren G.
  as U.S. president,
    17, 80–81
Harper's Weekly,
  47
Harvey, George, 47
Hitler, Adolf, 17
Huerta, Victoriano,
  55
Hughes, Charles Evan
  and the election of
    1916, 63

International Review,
  29
Italy, 56
  attack on Ethiopia,
    16
  and the Paris Peace
    Conference, 70–
    71
  and World War I,
    59

Japan, 64

Jefferson, Thomas
  and the Louisiana
    Purchase, 7
  and the revolution
    against the British,
    7
Johns Hopkins Univer-
  sity, 32–34, 90
Johnson, Andrew
  as U.S. president,
    24

Kennedy, David M.,
  82
Kennedy, John F.
  as U.S. president,
    82

League of Nations
  and Wilson, 11–12,
    15–17, 35, 56, 66,
    68, 71, 73–75,
    78–80, 82–83,
    89–90
Lee, Robert E., 22, 24
Lincoln, Abraham, 22
  as wartime president,
    7
Lodge, Henry Cabot,
  78
Louisiana Purchase,
  7–8
Lusitania (British ship)
  German bombing of,
    61–62

Madero, Francisco,
  55
Madison, James
  and the revolution
    against the British,
    7
Maine (battleship), 37

Marshall, Thomas R.
  as vice president,
    89
McKinley, William
  as U.S. president,
    37
Mexico, 23, 63–64, 90
  turmoil in, 54–55,
    60
Middleton, Connecti-
  cut, 35
Morgan, J.P., 41
Monroe, James
  as U.S. president,
    87
Montenegro, 72

New Jersey, 12, 47, 90
  and city commis-
    sioners, 49
  and Correct Practices
    Act, 49
  and direct primary
    system, 48
  and public utilities
    commission, 49
  and workmen's
    compensation law,
    49
Nobel Peace Prize
  and Wilson, 10–11,
    15, 80, 91

Orlando, Vittorio
  and the Paris Peace
    Conference, 71–
    72
Oslo, Norway, 12,
  91
Overland Monthly,
  31
Oxford University,
  42

INDEX

Panama Canal, 60
Paris Peace Confer-
  ence, 68–72
  and the "Big Four,"
  70–71
Patton, Francis L.
  as president of
    Princeton Univer-
    sity, 35, 40–41
Pershing, John J., 55
Philadelphia, Pennsyl-
  vania, 19
Pitt, William, 29
Presidents of the
  United States,
  84–88
  and the Constitu-
    tion, 86
  fact file of, 86–88
  powers of, 8, 86
  and the Presidential
    Seal, 88
  and tradition, 87
  and the White
    House, 88
Princeton University,
  28, 35–43, 90
"Princeton in the
  Nation's Service,"
  40
Progressive Party,
  50

Reagan, Ronald
  as wartime president,
  87
Republican Party, 48,
  50, 52, 60, 63, 80
Rockefeller, John D.,
  45
Romania, 57
Rome, Georgia, 31–
  32

Roosevelt, Franklin
  Delano
  as wartime president,
  7, 37, 80, 82, 87
Roosevelt, Theodore,
  41, 62
  and the election of
  1912, 50, 52
Russia, 56, 70, 78
  and World War I, 13,
  59, 68, 90

Schmedeman, Albert
  G., 12
Scotland, 19
Serbia
  and World War I,
  57–59, 72
Smith, Gene, 17
Smith, James E., 48
Smith, James S., 47
Socialist Party, 52, 78
Spanish-American War
  of 1898, 13, 37
State, The, 34
Staunton, Virginia,
  18–19, 21, 89–90

Taft, William Howard
  and the election of
  1912, 49–50, 52
  as wartime president,
  87
Thompson, William,
  41
Trenton, New Jersey,
  47
Truman, Harry S.
  as U.S. president, 8,
  80, 88
Turkey
  and World War I,
  59

Twain, Mark, 41

Underwood, Oscar W.
  and the election of
  1912, 52
Underwood Tariff Act,
  54
United Nations, 16,
  56, 68, 80, 83
United States of
  America
  government
    branches of, 9
  industrial powers of,
    44–47
  and the Paris Peace
    Conference, 70–
    71
  railroad system of,
    44, 79
  and social reform,
    45–48, 62, 77,
    79
  and wartime, 8, 55
  and World War I,
    13–14, 59, 61–65,
    68, 90
United States
  Congress, 8, 11,
  13–14, 30, 60, 64,
  66, 70, 78–80,
  86–87, 90
United States Consti-
  tution, 8–9, 29
  18th Amendment
    to, 74
  19th Amendment
    to, 76
  and presidency
    requirements, 7,
    86–87
University of Virginia,
  29–30

Versailles Treaty, 11, 72, 75, 77–80, 91
and the end of World War I, 15
Villa, Pancho, 55
Vinson, Fred, 8
Virginia, 20, 29

Walworth, Arthur, 21, 38
Washington, Booker T., 41
Washington, D.C., 12, 34, 63, 74, 79, 81, 83, 91
as U.S. capital, 88–89
Washington, George
as U.S. president, 87–88
and the revolution against the British, 7
Wilson's biography on, 40
Wesleyan University, 35, 37, 90
Wilmington, North Carolina, 28
Wilson, Annie (sister), 18
Wilson, Edith Galt (wife), 89
as first lady, 80–81
marriage of, 63, 69
Wilson, Eleanor (daughter), 89
birth of, 35
wedding of, 59
Wilson, Ellen Axson (wife), 30–31, 35, 41, 89
and Bright's disease, 59–60

death of, 60
as first lady, 53–54
marriage of, 31–33, 90
Wilson, James (grandfather), 18–19
Wilson, Janet "Jessie" (mother), 18, 20, 89
Wilson, Jessie (daughter), 89
birth of, 33
Wilson, Joseph Ruggles (father), 18, 25, 32, 89
as Presbyterian minister, 20–21, 24, 26, 28
Wilson, Joseph Jr. (brother), 18
Wilson, Margaret (daughter), 89
birth of, 33
Wilson, Marion (sister), 18
Wilson, Mary Anne Adams (grandmother), 18–19
Wilson Quarterly, 81
Wilson, (Thomas) Woodrow
achievements of, 54–55
as author, 31, 33–34, 38, 40, 42, 80, 90
birth, 19, 21, 89–90
early years of, 18–29
education of, 25–29, 90
and the election of 1912, 49–52
and the election of 1916, 63
death of, 81, 83, 89, 91

doctorate of, 34, 80
and foreign affairs, 60
Fourteen Points program of, 10, 65–67
as governor of New Jersey, 12, 48–49, 54, 89
illnesses of, 27, 31, 60, 78–79, 91
inaugural address of, 64
as lawyer, 30–31, 89–90
and the League of Nations, 11–12, 15–17, 35, 56, 66, 68–69, 71, 73–75, 78–80, 82–83, 89–90
marriages of, 31–33, 63, 69, 90
"New Freedom" platform, 52
and the Nobel Peace Prize, 10–11, 15, 80, 91
as orator, 38–40, 42, 48, 82
and the Paris Peace Conference, 68–72
and politics, 12, 17, 26, 28, 30, 43, 47–55
as president of Princeton University, 12, 36, 41–45, 47, 90
as (wartime) president of the U.S., 7, 10, 13, 37, 52–81, 87, 90

as professor, 12,
30–43, 80, 89–90
religious faith of, 26
as "Schoolmaster in
Politics," 80, 89
and social reform,
13, 45–48, 52, 62,
79
and the Versailles
Treaty, 12, 72,
77–80, 91
world peace vision
of, 10–17, 35,
37,56, 66, 68–69,

71, 73–75, 78–80,
83
and World War I, 80,
83, 89–90
Woodrow, Thomas
(grandfather), 20
Woodrow Wilson
House, 89
Woodrow Wilson
International Center
for Scholars, 80–81,
89
Woodrow Wilson Pres-
idential Library, 89

World War I, 11–13,
16, 59–66, 77, 80, 83,
89–90
the Allies in, 59, 65,
68
Armistice Day, 68
the Central Powers
in, 59
start of, 57, 60
World War II, 17, 37,
80

Yugoslavia, 72

PICTURE CREDITS

ACKNOWLEDGMENTS

Thank you to Celebrity Speakers Intl. for coordinating Mr. Cronkite's contribution to this book.

Ann Gaines is a freelance author who lives outside of Gonzales, Texas. She holds master's degrees in American civilization and library science from the University of Texas at Austin. She has written more than 50 nonfiction books for children, including other biographies for Chelsea House.

Walter Cronkite has covered virtually every major news event during his more than 60 years in journalism, during which he earned a reputation for being "the most trusted man in America." He began his career as a reporter for the United Press during World War II, taking part in the beachhead assaults of Normandy and covering the Nuremberg trials. He then joined *CBS News* in Washington, D.C., where he was the news anchor for political convention and election coverage from 1952 to 1980. CBS debuted its first half-hour weeknight news program with Mr. Cronkite's interview of President John F. Kennedy in 1963. Mr. Cronkite was inducted into the Academy of Television Arts and Sciences in 1985 and has written several books. He lives in New York City with his wife of 63 years.